ATTACK EVIL THAT IS ATTACKING YOU

A MANUAL FOR DELIVERANCE
By
Fr. Francis Pompei Ofm

Copyright
All rights reserved

No part of this publication may be reproduced, stored in a retrieval system or transmitted in any form or by any means, mechanical, electronic, photocopying, recording or otherwise without the prior written permission of the publisher.

INTRODUCTION

Unfortunately, many Christians do not know they have been given the power and means to deliver themselves and others from attacks and temptations from Satan, Evil Spirits, and Powers.

- **"Deliver us from Evil"... (Mt. 6:13)**

- **"These are the signs that will follow all believers... They will cast out devils." (Mk. 16:17-20)**

Because many have not been taught this, they are either afraid of Satan and Evil, or they deny its existence. That's why Evil keeps winning, because there are fewer and fewer believers who oppose, attack, and cast them out.

Finally, you have the answer from Jesus, but not only the answer, but what to do and how to do it. The following Manual contains Rituals for you to use the power of the Lord to start winning and torture the Evil that brought Sin, Suffering, and Death into the world, to you and your loved ones.

*When you see **JESUS:** this is Jesus personally talking and teaching You.

TABLE OF CONTENTS

CHAPTER 1   **PG 4**
Origins Of Evil And The Corruption And Destruction Of Our Bodies And Minds

CHAPTER 2   **PG 17**
How Evil Has Infected Humanity And Physical Reality With Suffering And Death

CHAPTER 3   **PG 30**
How Spirits and Demons Can enter you

CHAPTER 4   **PG 37**
Attacking Evil and Winning

CHAPTER 5   **PG 45**
Exorcism in the Catholic Church

CHAPTER 6   **PG 51**
Deliverance Rituals

CHAPTER 7   **PG 67**
Final Thoughts when you Pray a Deliverance

CREDITS   **PG 75**

CHAPTER 1
ORIGINS OF EVIL AND THE CORRUPTION AND DESTRUCTION OF OUR BODIES AND MINDS

Let's be clear. Suffering has the most questions that need answers, not only for you and me, but for all humanity. Before the Lord answers your questions about Suffering and Death, I want to put some flesh and blood on the word 'suffering' so you will get the scope and depth of it and feel its overwhelming power on your thoughts, feelings, and emotions.

- Cancer; heart failure; Alzheimer's disease; mental illness; mutations; chronic pain; chronic nausea; severe arthritis; spine injury; eating disorders; lung disease; stomach and bowel pain and disorders; chronic migraine headaches; innocent babies, infants, children, suffering and dying in the arms of their parents; somebody's daughter abducted, raped, dismembered, and thrown away like trash.

- Terrorism; beheading; torture; genocide; drug addiction; human trafficking; capturing young kids, girls, and women to rape, sell, enslave, and then butcher and kill; school shootings; wars; bombing; biochemical warfare; mutilation; suffocation; water boarding; abortion; partial birth abortion.

Sadly enough, it probably did not take long for you to read the above list and experience the Evil power that Fear has over us. I don't know about you, but I have a hard time digesting and wrapping my head around the whole thing. When it comes to the depth, darkness and despair that Evil attacks us with, it can be overwhelming and even terrifying. I created this list of questions to introduce the devastating destruction evil has brought upon humanity, you and me, and that is Suffering.

- Where did it come from? Why do we have to suffer?

- Why do little babies have to suffer and die? They are innocent and did nothing wrong.

- Why does God allow it?

- Why do we suffer and have to die?

- If God really loves us, why doesn't He do something about it?

- If Jesus came to save us from all this Sin, Suffering and Death, where is it, and where is He when we pray?

The bottom line is this. If there is no difference or change in Sin, Suffering and Death since Jesus came, why should anyone believe in him as a loving God? What is the use, really?

Many times, these lingering questions are the reasons for believers leaving the church, faith, and religion all together. Without answers, part of me does not blame them.

EVIL AND SUFFERING: FINALLY, THE ANSWERS:

How did suffering and death enter the world, affecting all of us & all physical reality?

God does not cause Suffering and Death. EVIL does. How did Evil come into the world and all physical reality? Every major religion, society, and culture has discussed and debated the answer to this question. They have even written about it in their sacred texts. I find that the most detailed and credible texts regarding Evil's origin are from the **Book of Enoch.**

The book of Enoch, found in Qumran in 1948 near the Dead Sea, though not in the Canonical inspired books of the Bible, is one of the oldest of the Creation narratives. The Book of Genesis in the Judeo-Christian Bible borrows much from the Book of Enoch. For our purposes, here is an English overview and translation of the passage describing how Evil came into the world.

BOOK OF ENOCH (A brief overview)

In the Book of Enoch, the "Watchers" are angels dispatched to Earth to watch over the humans. They soon begin to lust for human women and at the prodding of their leader Samyaza (Leader of Fallen Angels), they defect to illicitly instruct humanity and procreate with them. The offspring of these unions are the Nephilim, savage giants who pillage the earth and endanger humanity.

Samyaza and his associates further taught their human charges arts and technologies such as weaponry, cosmetics, mirrors, sorcery, and other techniques that would otherwise be discovered gradually over time by humans, not foisted upon them all at once.

Eventually God allows a Great Flood to rid the earth of the Nephilim, but first sends the Archangel Uriel to warn Noah so as not to eradicate the human race. The Watchers are bound "in the valleys of the Earth" until **Judgment Day when they will be released and then cast into Hell forever**.

BOOK OF ENOCH

"And when their sons have slain one another, and they have seen the destruction of their beloved ones, bind them fast for seventy generations in the bowels of the earth, until the day of their Judgment. In those days, they shall be lead away to the abyss of fire, and to the torment and the prison, in which they shall be confined forever.

Whosoever shall be condemned and destroyed will from henceforth be bound together with them to the end of all generations and destroy all the spirits of the reprobate and the children of the Watchers, because they have wronged mankind. Destroy all wrong from the face of the earth, and let every evil work come to an end: and let the plant of righteousness and truth appear, and it shall prove a blessing; the works of righteousness and truth shall be planted in truth and joy for evermore.

Enoch, thou scribe of righteousness, go and declare to the Watchers of the Heaven, who have left the high Heaven, the holy eternal place. They have defiled themselves with women, have done as the children of earth do, and have taken unto themselves wives, "Ye have wrought great destruction on the earth, and ye shall have no peace, nor forgiveness of sin, and as they delight themselves in their children, the murder of their beloved ones shall they see.

Over the destruction of their children shall they lament and shall make supplication unto eternity, but mercy and peace shall ye not attain." (Book of Enoch, chapters 6, 7, 8)

Enoch describes the chronology of Satan and the fallen angels. It illustrates what they chose and did to their estate in Heaven, their relationship with God, and to us.

The following are Scriptures that describe the essence of God, who is mystery, yet revealed with His own words. What is important is that all reality in the Spirit World as well as the physical, including you and me, shares in the **Unconditional Love** and **Light** that is God. By reflecting on God as Light, we can appreciate who and what we are to God and understand the magnitude of what Satan and the fallen angels lost and can never get back. It is interesting that one of the names associated with Satan and Evil is Lucifer, which means Light.

Put simply, in choosing to be 'God' and have his own kingdom, power, and servants (humanity), who Satan and his fallen angels would corrupt, control, and manipulate with knowledge of Good and Evil, lost their Light and the Unconditional Love of God. As you read the following Scriptures, it will become clear that **God is Light,** and all

Creation, you and me, share in His light. We are beings of Light, but because of what Evil has done to us, there is now darkness, Sin, Suffering and Death.

LIGHT AND DARKNESS: WE ARE LIGHT MADE PHYSICAL

- "**GOD IS LIGHT**, in him there is no darkness at all." Note we are not told that God is a light, but that HE IS LIGHT. Light is His essence, as is Unconditional Love. (1 Jn. 5)

- Jesus told them, "You are going to have the light just a little while longer. Walk while you have the light before darkness overtakes you. Whoever walks in the dark does not know where they are going." (Jn. 12:35)

- "Believe in the light while you have the light, so that you may become children of light." (Jn. 12:36)

- "This is the message we have heard from him and declare to you, God is light; in Him, there is no darkness at all." (1 Jn. 1:5)

- When Jesus spoke again to the people, He said, "I am the light of the world. Whoever follows me will never walk in darkness, but will have the light of life." (Jn. 8:12)

- "If we do not have the light, we do not know God.

Those who know God, who walk with Him, are of the light and walk in the light. They are partakers of God's divine nature, having escaped the corruption in the world caused by evil desires." (2 Peter 1:4)

- "God is light, and so is His Son." Jesus said, I am the 'Light of the world'. You are all children of the light and children of the day. We do not belong to the night or to the darkness."(1 Thessalonians 5:5)

- "As adopted sons of God, we are to reflect His light into a world darkened by sin. Our goal in witnessing to the unsaved is "to open their eyes and turn them from darkness to light and from the power of Satan to God." (Acts 26:18)

To help clarify what all this means in the big picture for you and me, run this through your Mind. Every day it is the choice between **Physical Reality** (The World and the Flesh as Jesus referred to it, subject to our human desires, Sin, Suffering, and Death) and The Spirit, **God's light**. I cannot say it any better than God did

"I place before you "Life and Death." Choose Life!"
(Deut. 30)

SUMMARY:

- God did not create Evil. Conscious spiritual beings, created by God in Heaven were sent to guide and live among humanity—angels. They lusted after human women, seduced and had sex with them, which was forbidden by God both for humans and the fallen angels. These spiritual beings in physical bodies wanted to be "gods," having their own Kingdom and followers. Because they had knowledge greater than ours, they interfered with our DNA through sex and genetic engineering; cloning; cross breeding; producing evil monsters who taught knowledge to humans that God forbade.

"We were created a little less than the angels..."
(Hebrews 2:7)

Thus, Evil came into the physical realm permanently and with it, Suffering and Death. If this sounds like a Science fiction movie and fantasy story (Myth), it may not be anymore, because of recent archeological and scientific discoveries.

- We now can manipulate chromosomes and DNA.

- We now can mix different DNAs to create new species.

- We now are on the cutting edge of artificial intelligence. We now can clone a human body.

- We are developing mind control techniques

Maybe what the Theologians and Scripture scholars thought was a myth, little by little, may become actual recorded history. Remember, I am only speculating here, because of recent discoveries that strongly suggest the possibility.

I find the Book of Enoch the most credible description of the origin of Evil that describes not just as myths and stories but actual recorded historical events. This should wake up theologians and Scripture scholars who are reading this and are loaded to dispute The Book of Enoch as a historical narrative.

My purpose in writing this book is not to give a definitive answer to the Origin of Evil, rather that they are conscious beings with knowledge, power, and realities that exist, affect, and influence us.

WHAT JESUS SAID ABOUT SATAN AND EVIL

- "A Liar & The father of Lies"   Jn. 8:44
- "A murderer"   Jn. 8:44
- "The Tempter"   Mt. 4:3
- "The Prince of Demons"   Mt. 12:24
- "He perverts the Scripture"   Mt. 4:4
- "The god of this world"   2Cor. 4:4
- "The Deceiver of the World"   Rev. 12:9
- "The Seducer of Adam and Eve"   Gen. 3:1-20
- "He has a Kingdom"   Mt. 12:26
- "Evil men are his sons"   Mt. 13:38
- "Eternal fire is prepared for him" Mt. 25
- "Seeks to devour believers"   1 Peter 5
- "The Enemy- The Evil One"   Mt. 13:39

CONCLUSION:

- Does the devil and Evil really exist? The language of Jesus certainly indicates his own belief in the existence of a personal devil.

- Satan and Evil have affected, rather infected, all of physical reality, which includes our physical bodies—brain included.

- Evil can infest our MINDS with thoughts and images that awaken our emotions, feelings, desires, passions, and affect our choices, if we let it. Evil, ultimately intends to seduce, control, enslave, destroy us, and use us to destroy each other.

Take a moment to read the above three conclusions and remember them. Why? You cannot defeat the Enemy, unless you know who they are, and how they operate.

According to Jesus and the New Testament, Satan and Evil exists, Conscious beings with divine knowledge have powers. If you do not believe in this, remember your problem is not with me, but with Jesus.

- "The one who does what is sinful is of the devil, because the devil has been sinning from the beginning. The reason the Son of God appeared was to destroy the devil's work." (1 Jn. 3:8)

- "I am afraid that just as Eve was deceived by the

serpent's cunning, your minds may somehow be led astray from your sincere and pure devotion to Christ." (2 Corinthians 11:3)

- "Submit yourselves then to God. Resist the devil, and he will flee from you." (James 4:7)

If all this Satan and Evil talk is starting to frighten you, relax, because there is not only good but Great News coming. By the time you finish this book, Satan and Evil will be frightened and terrified of YOU.

EVIL EXPOSED: HOW IT AFFECTS OUR MINDS

To recapitulate, we know that Evil exists and its intention when it comes to all physical reality. That is, it is to ultimately destroy God's creation and humanity, including You and Me. Now we can unmask its powers, how it operates and affects our minds and bodies. If the only thing Evil can do is put thoughts and images in your minds, then your Mind is the battlefield where you are in continual warfare with Evil that is trying to seduce, control your Will and decisions, and ultimately destroy you and all of us.

SCRIPTURE: REGARDING YOUR MIND

Romans 12:2
- "Do not be conformed to this world but be transformed by the renewal of your mind, that by testing, you may discern what is the will of God, what is good and acceptable and perfect."

Corinthians 2:13-16
- "We impart this in words not taught by human wisdom, but taught by the Spirit, interpreting spiritual truths to those who are spiritual. The natural person does not accept the things of the Spirit of God, for they are folly to him, and he is not able to understand them, because they are spiritually discerned. The spiritual person judges all things but himself to be judged by no one. For who has understood the mind of the Lord so as to instruct him, but **we have the mind of Christ.**

Timothy 1:7
- "For God gave us a spirit not of fear, but of power, love, and self-control."

Jesus is teaching us that, in fact, we are in school, and He is retraining our Minds to think and operate the way His does. This is not a "one time deal," but takes a whole lifetime to learn and get better at it. The good news is the more we do it, the better we get, and the more natural it becomes.

The point here is that the Lord is telling you what to do and how to do it every day. The more you replace the negative thoughts, images, half-truths, and lies that Evil and the world infest your mind with every day, the more you will feel the freedom from your fear and worrying.

"Finally, brothers, whatever is true, whatever is honorable, whatever is just, whatever is pure, whatever is lovely, whatever is commendable, if there is any excellence, if there is anything worthy of praise, think about these things." (Phil. 4:8)

"Do not be Afraid or let your hearts be troubled. Trust in the Father and Trust in Me. The power in YOU is truly greater that the evil powers, principalities, and demons that are in the world. Learn to not only believe this, but to use this power and attack evil whenever it is attacking. I am and will be there to punish and cast it out together with you."

CHAPTER 2
HOW EVIL HAS INFECTED HUMANITY AND PHYSICAL REALITY WITH SUFFERING AND DEATH

"All of Creation Groans for the Salvation of the Lord"

HOW EVIL WORKS: PAY CLOSE ATTENTION!

Evil puts thoughts and images in your mind, tempting you to choose, download, and think about them. When you choose to think about them, that is when powers and spirits can almost immediately enter your feelings, emotions and desires, with fear, anxiety, lust, anger, etc.

When you continue to DWELL on them, they intensify your emotions and desires to act on them. This can lead to obsession, when you cannot stop your mind from thinking about and dwelling on your problems or suffering. This is like putting gasoline on the fire of your passions and desires.

Then you become like a volcano ready to erupt and the only way to release these desires and emotions is to act on them and do the Evil that promises you pleasure and satisfaction. When you succumb to this temptation and attack, you choose (Your WILL) to do the Evil.

It's like a computer. I hope you are a little computer savvy. If you are, then you have probably seen the irritating blue screen with the message that your computer is infected with a virus. Doesn't it frustrate you? And it usually happens when you are right in the middle of something important.

Next is that little icon at the bottom of the screen that starts pulsating, and the following message pops up: "Your computer is infected with a Virus. Click here and download a free program that will clean your hard drive from the virus." Here is the question for you, should you click on the free anti- virus program that promises to restore your computer? If you are computer literate, your answer is **NO**. Why, because **it is the VIRUS**.

This is exactly how Evil works on our Minds. It promises you everything, but in the end destroys you and others. Evil has power over us while we are in these physical bodies, because they have not only interfered with our DNA physically, but also our Minds and infected them with the capacity to 'know' and experience Good and Evil.

This is one of the reasons Jesus came to save us, that is, to give us authority and power over Evil. The only problem is that many clergy and religious leaders never taught us about Jesus' power to deliver and how to do it. The good news here is that Jesus will teach you how, later in this Manual. Be patient, He will do this later and then do it with you. Now that is something to get excited about and look forward to!

St. Paul describes the battle that goes on in our minds and how Evil has power over us.

- "I know that the law is spiritual; but I am unspiritual

sold as a slave to sin. I do not understand what I do. For what I want to do I do not do, but what I hate I do. If I do what I do not want to do, I agree that the law is good, as it is no longer I who do it, but it is sin living in me.

- For I know that good itself does not dwell in me, that is, in my sinful nature. I have the desire to do what is good, but I cannot carry it out.

- For I do not do the good I want to do, but the Evil I do not want to do—this I keep on doing. Now if I do what I do not want to do, it is no longer I who do it, but it is sin living in me that does it.

- Therefore, I find this law at work, although I want to do Good, Evil is right there with me. For in my inner being I delight in God's law; but I see another law at work in me, waging war against the law of my mind and making me a prisoner of the law of sin at work within me.

- What a wretched man I am! Who will rescue me from this body, that is subject to death? **Praise to my Lord Jesus Christ, for in Him there is no condemnation.** (Rom. 8:1)

Let us take this and apply how Evil works on our minds, with an issue of the day. The following is an article I wrote and submitted to a local newspaper.

EXAMPLE: IDENTITY POLITICS

My greatest fear is that Identity Politics has led us to divisions, not only in our political views, but in our churches, communities, and what's worse: in our families and with our friends. From division, Identity Politics has led to anger and then to violent anger that wants to retaliate and punish. The more we engage in it, the more we become obsessed by it, demonize people, and are filled with hatred. The final choice is open harassment, violence, and then civil war.

I believe the power and forces that are driving this are not just part of our human nature, but demonic. Evil is the one word that is mentioned often, but never discussed, understood, or addressed how it seduces, influences, and then controls people's minds, will, and actions. Maybe it is time to not only discuss answers and solutions to the issues, but also the evil forces that are the real enemy influencing, obsessing and possessing terrorists, rapists, murderers, traffickers, gangs, and even ourselves.

In the Christian Scripture it says, "Our struggle is not against flesh and blood, but against the rulers, principalities and powers of this dark world and the spiritual forces of Evil in the heavenly realms." (Eph. 6:12) The reason Evil seems to be triumphing is that most people do not believe in Satan or Evil powers. Not a bad tactic on Satan's part to keep people powerless by their choice to not believe, while He's busy achieving his ends without any resistance.

Politicians, media, news networks and their "so called" professional panels, debates and "reliable" sources have produced NO answers or solutions but only division and have given birth to their evil child: Identity Politics.

Identity Politics is merely the "politically correct" term for hate and demonizing those who disagree with us. The hidden and inherent evil in identity politics is the **Self-Righteous Justification** Evil uses to, little by little, control our minds with negative thoughts, half- truths and lies that overwhelm and drive us to verbal and physical violence.

Evil is the real enemy, but for the most part no one wants to talk about it and those that do are considered out of touch with reality. Yet, Satan and Evil, or whatever you call them have existed and been experienced from the beginning of humanity and recorded in every major and ancient Religion.

Evil does not need our belief in it to exist. It does exist and my guess is that most of us have heard, seen, or experienced something that seemed so surreal that our minds were unable to comprehend it. And we recoiled in terror because it was beyond human. Because we do not acknowledge its existence, we give it free reign to influence our minds, will, and actions.

Personally, I am tired of politics, media, news networks, panels, experts, Republicans and Democrats. I'm tired of narratives, and most of all I'm tired of words, words, and more words that Identity Politics offers—words that fuel demonizing people, hatred, and violence.

This is my attempt to expose the real enemy, Evil, and what it has done and is doing to people and humanity. My prayer is that this will be a "wake up" call for all of us tempted and seduced by Identity Politics. Let's cross the divide, close ranks and focus only on finding real answers and solutions for real people. My hope is to begin the conversation to understand and call out Evil and develop a strategy to combat and cast it out of our conversations. This article demonstrates how Evil, by our choosing to download, think about, and dwell on the thoughts and images it puts in our minds, progresses to a point where we are driven to act on them—ultimately destroying ourselves and maybe others.

I categorize these Evil thoughts into:

- **NEGATIVE THOUGHTS:** Doctor: "I'm sorry, but your tests came back positive."

- **HALF-TRUTHS:** "You are terminal and going to die."

- **LIES:** "Death is the end of your existence and life."

CASTING OUT' EVIL THOUGHTS FROM YOUR MIND

Using the analogy of **NOT** clicking on and downloading the free program to delete the virus in your computer, because it is the **Virus, don't download** the evil thoughts or images.

HERE ARE THE STEPS OF WHAT TO DO:

1. Say **NO** the minute you become aware that you are afraid or being tempted and seduced. Use your **WILL** and choose to say NO.

2. Then Say, **'LORD'**, the same as you did the minute you experienced a problem or suffering when you were four years old and cried out for Mommy. This step is not magic, but the most difficult of all, and the essential element to getting your degree in Trust. You are using your **WILL** to say **'NO'** and choosing to focus off the negative thoughts, half-truths and lies and on Jesus right there with you.

3. Evil is not going to give up attacking and tempting you, especially when it has successfully trained your mind for years to download everything into your mind and immediately think about and dwell on them. In this step, you will need to say **NO** many times, and probably for the rest of your earthly life, because this is the way the Lord will retrain your Mind.

EXAMPLE:

The doctor tells you that the results of your tests are positive for cancer. This is a serious **negative** thought, right? If you choose to download and think about it, immediately a flood of more half-truths and lies enter like, "Its terminal, I know it. I'm going to die. It's the end of my life; what about my family?"

Then the images of suffering download and "How am I going to deal with this? I can't do it." Does this sound familiar? And the worst is yet to come—**Fear**. The more you choose to think and dwell on those incoming thoughts and images the more intense they get. Your emotions and feelings kick in almost instantly, and Fear turns into terror as you see there is no way out. Your mind keeps racing and racing out of control.

It is at this point that people of faith pray and ask God to help them to make the problem go away, be healed and put to rest. If they keep praying and praying, and the cancer or problem does not go away, gets worse, and death is imminent—the next lie of Evil is "You're wasting your time praying and going to church. If God really loved you like He said, He would heal you."

This is 'the moment of truth' for you and your relationship with Jesus. Are you going to Trust Him no matter what, or are you going to succumb to the Fear and Evil's lies that are tempting you to Doubt. If you choose to Doubt and stop trusting in the Lord, Evil will lead you into the dark hole of despair with only your problem and without hope. This is, as I said before, the goal of Evil—to destroy you and keep you from the power of the Lord and the Truth.

Focusing on the Lord with you is an act of Trust, which is what we are here in school to learn and grow in.

JESUS:
"Remember when I said that the TRUTH will set you free? I meant it. I myself am the Truth, the Way, and the Life. The Truth you seek is not just a thought, but an experience of My love for you, so read and memorize the Truth about

anger, suffering, guilt, and death. Then memorize Evil's lies, and from now on say **NO** to them, reject them, do not let them in. Instead, focus on the Truth and me until you are able to set yourself free from fear. Stay with me, like you did when you were a child and ran to your mother for her strength and love.

Keep reading, because there is more good news to come. Replace the negative thoughts, half-truths, and lies with the TRUTH."

EXERCISE: Take your time when reading the Truths to replace those evil thoughts that are at the root of much of your suffering. Memorize them, burn the Truth in your mind and use the truth to counteract the evil thoughts.

FEAR/ANGER/DOUBT/DESPAIR

LIES-HALF-TRUTHS- NEGATIVE THOUGHTS:
- Death is the End.
- The tests will be positive— I know it. I'll never endure this.
- Why is God punishing me?
- What's the use of praying? God isn't doing anything.

TRUTH: Jesus, what do you say?
- "Don't be afraid or let your hearts be troubled. Trust

in God and trust in Me." (Jn. 14:27)

- "I am with you every day until the end of time." (Mt. 28:20) "Where there is fear, love has not been perfected, love dispels fear." (1 Jn. 4:18)

- "While you are in the world you will suffer (and your bodies will die), but don't be afraid, for I overcame my fear of Suffering and Death and will be with you in yours." (Jn. 16:33)

GUILT/SELF-HATRED

LIES-HALF-TRUTHS- NEGATIVE THOUGHTS:
- I hurt others deeply. I am selfish and destroyed someone and myself.

- I can never get back what I lost. God could never forgive me. I am embarrassed, ashamed, and just want to hide. I'm going to hell. This feeling of guilt will never go away, no matter what I do. I don't like myself for what I did. I don't think I can live with this every day, for the rest of my life.

TRUTH:
- To the woman caught in adultery, Jesus said: "Does anyone condemn you, then neither do I condemn you. Go and sin no more." (Jn. 8)

- What I do, I do not understand, for I do not do what I want, but what I hate. For I do not do the good I want, but I do the Evil I do not want. Because I am a slave to sin, what a wretched man I am! Who will deliver me from this mortal body? "Praise be my Lord Jesus Christ for those who are in Him, there is NO condemnation!" (Romans 8)

- The Prodigal Father never asked his son who returned home what he did or what his sins were. He said, "Put rings on his fingers, give him a cloak, kill the fatted calf, and let's celebrate. (Lk. 15)

- The Lord unconditionally loves you before you sin, while you are sinning, and after. His love for you never changes. Look at a Crucifix and you'll see it.

SUFFERING

LIES-HALF-TRUTHS- NEGATIVE THOUGHTS:
- I will never be able to go through it.

- It will always hurt this badly and get even worse. Where is God, and why me?

- I won't be able to do the things I use to. What's the use of living?

- It is so frustrating. Will it ever stop?

- I don't understand why we have to suffer for so long. Life is hell.

TRUTH:
- "Therefore, we are not discouraged; rather, although

our outer self (physical body) is wasting away, our inner self is being renewed day by day." (2 Cor. 4:16)

- "For this momentary suffering is producing for us an eternal glory beyond all comparison, as we look not to what is seen but to what is unseen; for what is seen is transitory, but what is unseen is eternal." (2 Cor. 4:18) "The sufferings of the present are as nothing, compared to the Glory that will be revealed in us." (Rom. 8:18-23) "While you are in the World you will suffer, but don't be afraid, for I overcame the world….and I am with you every day, until the end of time." (Jn. 16:13)

- "If we share and experience the sufferings of Christ, we will share in His resurrection." (Rom. 8:17)

DEATH

LIES- HALF-TRUTHS- NEGATIVE THOUGHTS:
- I am dying. It is the end of my life, dead, forgotten, wake, funeral, and buried.

- I will never see my loved ones or experience joy and happiness again.

- I can't stop thinking about it, and I'm afraid of the suffering ahead and my life ending.

- This is it. I'm never getting out of this one. What is going to happen to my family and loved ones?

- I am so frightened and feel so alone and abandoned by God.

TRUTH:
- "Our Citizenship and Home is in Heaven, and from it we also await a Savior, the Lord Jesus Christ." (Phil. 3:20)

- "I am the Resurrection and the Life. Anyone who believes in me will never die, and anyone who dies believing in me will live forever. (Jn. 11:25)

- We can't even begin to imagine how great will be the Glory that the Lord will manifest in us." (Rom. 8:18)

- "For if we have been united with him in a death like his, we will certainly be united with him in His resurrection. (Rom. 6:5)

- "Do not let your hearts be troubled. Have faith in God; have faith in me. In my Father's house, there are many dwelling places. I will come back again and take you to myself, so that where I am, you also may be." (Jn. 14:1)

CHAPTER 3
HOW DEMONS AND SPIRITS CAN ENTER YOU

So far you have learned how Satan and Evil puts thoughts and images in our minds that tempt and seduce us.

It is of the utmost importance that you read slowly, reflect on, and do a survey of your life to understand how you may have willingly or unwillingly allowed Evil Spirits, Powers, and Demons into your mind, body, and seduce your Will.

This is serious territory and many churches have neglected to talk about the Occult, Evil rituals, and practices that may seem innocent and entertaining, instead open the floodgate to Demons, Spirits and Principalities to enter our minds, attach to us, and torment us with the goal of eventually controlling and using us for their demonic intentions.

> **"St. Michael, help us always to resist the following, steadfast in the Faith."**

GOD'S WARNING AND CONDEMNATION

- "Let no one be found among you who sacrifices his son or daughter in the fire, who practices divination or sorcery, interprets omens, engages in witchcraft, or casts spells, or who is a Medium or who consults the dead. Anyone who does these things is detestable to the Lord, and because of these detestable practices the Lord your God will drive out those nations before you." (Deut. 18)

- Many of those who believed came and openly confessed their evil deeds. A number who had practiced **sorcery** brought their scrolls together and burned them publicly.

In this way the word of the Lord spread widely and grew in power. (Acts 19:18-20)

- Do not turn to Mediums or seek out Spiritualists, for you will be defiled by them. I am the LORD your God. (Leviticus 19:31)

- I will set my face against the person who turns to Mediums and Spiritualists to prostitute himself by following them, and I will cut him off from his people. (Leviticus 20:6)

- When men tell you to consult Mediums and Spiritualists, who whisper and mutter, should not a people inquire of their God? Why consult the dead on behalf of the living? (Isaiah 8:19)

ASTROLOGY

- And when you look up to the sky and see the sun, the moon and the star, all the heavenly array, do not be enticed into bowing down to them and worshiping things the LORD your God has apportioned to all the nations under heaven. (Deuteronomy 4:19)

- Do not practice divination or sorcery. (Leviticus 19:26)

- The idols speak deceit, Diviners see visions that lie; they tell dreams that are false, they give comfort in vain. Therefore the people wander like sheep oppressed for lack of a shepherd. (Zechariah 10:2)

FALSE GODS AND IDOLS

- You shall not make for yourself an idol in the form of anything in heaven above or on the earth beneath or in the waters below. You shall not bow down to them or worship them; for I, the LORD your God, am a jealous God, punishing the children for the sin of the fathers to the third and fourth generation of those who hate me. (Exodus 20:4-5)

SEANCES

Seances are occult Evil rituals and practices conducted by Mediums whose power is to contact the dead or persons who've crossed over to another level of reality. A séance means to "sit" with spirits from another world.

Sometimes Mediums hear otherworldly voices along with seeing spirits manifesting themselves from another world.

These Demons and Spirits can speak through the Medium or with the use of Ouija board or writing on an object.

TRUST ME, it's not your 'Uncle Tanoose' who's voice you're hearing, but a Demon or Spirit that is mimicking your Uncle.

DIVINATION

Divination is the attempt to gain foresight and knowledge about the future through various methods. These are your fortune-tellers, Leaf or Palm readers, and Psychics who may use Crystal Balls and Tarot cards all for the sake of predicting events and telling your future. Once again you are opening yourself, mind, soul, and Will to the Spirit World other than the

Holy Spirit and the Lord. Say **NO** to this crap and to anybody who is or wants to get involved in it. Ouija boards and Tarot cards make good kindling for a fire. **Get to it!**

SATANISM

Satanic cults have been officially documented in Europe and North America as far back as the 17th century.

The Satanic Church was established in America in the 1960s. These Cults/Churches are worldwide. The strange and violent practices, like black masses where a Catholic Consecrated Host (Eucharist-Body and Blood of Jesus) is stolen and desecrated with a woman's vagina.

In addition they are involved in bazaar orgies with children and adults and horrific sexual rituals and actions, murder, Human Sacrifice to Satan, including <u>suicide</u>. They appeal to the lowest and darkest parts of our fallen nature, mentioned in the Book of Enoch. Believe me when I say they are more prevalent than you think.

Remember Satan and Evil hates humanity, yet they want to **STEAL OUR LIGHT** which they lost and we still have because of Jesus. They ultimately want to make us their slaves and disciples by seducing us with the pleasure they give through unbridled sex, hatred, torture, and destroying others and God's creation.

EXAMPLE:

In the 1990s in the United States, there was the 'Vampire Cult', led by Rod Ferrell, who murdered a family in Florida using a horrific sadistic Sacrifice Ritual. Ferrell was only 16 years old at the time of the murders.

The news reported that this cult took drugs, performed blood and sex rituals and orgies, and later killed Naomi Ruth Queen and Richard Wendorf. Though rare, human sacrifice has definitely found its way into today's society, often as a Ritual to please Satan and experience other worldly pleasure when doing it. (Example Terrorists: Rape of children and beheadings)

Sounds like a science fiction movie, doesn't it, but tragically it is not. This is the battle between Good and Evil that the Lord gives us His power to confront. So, **DON'T BE AFRAID, REMEMBER WE WIN THE WAR**, and my hope is that this Manual will give you the Trust in the Lord and the Tools to win the battles, not just for yourself, but for others who are Evil's victims.

SPELLS

Spells are technically recitals, words spoken by a Wizard or one who has chosen and been given the power by evil to affect persons, places or things. Tokens, charms, combination of various plants and animal parts for a brew, to putting pins in a likeness of the person that the spell is cast on. The true power of the spell is in the recitation of certain ancient chants,

'Hocus Pocus" Crap

For ages, people have been using spells to unleash misfortune upon others, some for general bad luck and others for revenge and even something that will cause the death of their victims. Spells can be made to even affect sleep with demonic nightmares.

DEMONISM

Probably we have all seen movies where the Evil Bad Guy or Woman invoke the Gods and Specific Demons to give them power to conduct their actions, especially to torture, murder, or destroy.

Demonism seeks to summon the power of specific <u>Demons</u> to empower the petitioner to carry out their evil deeds. Since ancient times, occultists have believed that they can harness the power of these dark Spirits and Demons. Those who teach and practice Demonism use ritualistic incantations to summon different demons for various purposes in many cultures throughout history believed to be responsible for humanity's most violent acts. <u>Serial-killers</u> and brutal dictators have been thought to be under the control of these demonic influences, perhaps even causing most of humanity's atrocities.

ADD TO THIS:

- Certain Demonic Computer Games And Movies
- Witches Covens
- New Age Rituals
- Voodoo
- Santeria
- Drug Cults

Your reaction to all this may be one of doubt that this is really happening or write it off as psychological disorders and just a bunch of crazy people.

My response to you, as a Priest involved in the Deliverance Ministry is,

"They are real, exist, and these groups, people, and practices are RAMPANT, but operate in the background and secret lest they be discovered, brought into the Light and destroyed."

Because they are real and exist was and is my reason and motivation for writing this Manual so You **<u>WON'T</u>** be frightened of anything you have read so far, but instead, experience and use the power Jesus has given us to **ATTACK, PUNISH, BIND and CAST them OUT**.

My Response to this is

Halleluiah Jesus!!!!

CHAPTER 4
ATTACKING EVIL AND WINNING
What To Do And How To Do It!

Are you scared yet with all this talk about Satan and Evil? Is your Fear thermometer rising with thoughts that there just may be more than the Evil humanity and we generate?

According to what God said about Satan, Evil has and continues to corrupt humanity and all physical reality with the intention to tempt, experiment with, enslave, steal our Light, soul, consciousness, and ultimately destroy us.

I offer as proof that this is real by the Fear that enters your mind when you consider and think about Satan and Evil.

Why? **Fear** is Evil's greatest power.

I found the following article that will put some flesh and blood reality on what Satan and Evil are up to, according to the Word of God and what Jesus said about them.

Pay close attention to the following story that demonstrates that Evil not only **TEMPTS** us to Wrongdoing, but **SEDUCES** us with Good things and activities that we eventually **ADDICT** to.

This is the way Evil slowly influences our Will to **REPLACE GOD**, Church, and our Church family with our desires for things and activities that we want to do that give us pleasure, entertain us, power, and make us feel good.

KEEP THEM BUSY by Ralph Andrus

Satan called a worldwide convention of demons. In his opening address to his evil angels, he said, "We can't keep Christians from going to church. We cannot keep them from reading their Bibles and knowing the truth. We can't even keep them from holding onto their conservative values, but we can do something else. We can keep them from forming an intimate lasting relationship and experience with Christ. If they gain that connection with Jesus, our power over them is broken.

So, this is what I want you to do. I want you to distract them from experiencing Jesus Christ and having a personal relationship with Him, throughout their day. Let them go to church, let them have their conservative lifestyles, but steal their time so they cannot gain that experience and relationship with Jesus.

The Evil angels asked him, "How shall we do this?

- Keep them busy with the nonessentials of life to occupy their minds with more things to buy and more things to do. They'll not only be distracted, but addict to them, like sports, shopping, electronics, TV, and cell phones. This is how their addiction will replace God, their Church family and even ignore their friends and loved ones, too busy starring at their cell phones and tablets.

- Tempt them to spend, spend, then charge, charge, and charge it. Convince husbands and wives to work long hours and overtime so they can afford their lifestyles. This will keep them from spending time with their families and talking to Jesus.

- See to it that every store and restaurant in the world plays suggestive and seductive music, trashing Christian values. This will jam their minds and break their relationship with Jesus.

- Fill their coffee tables with magazines and newspapers. Pound their minds with the news 24 hours a day.

- Invade their driving moments with billboards. Flood their mailboxes with junk mail, sweepstakes, mail order catalogs and every kind of newsletter and promotion offering free products, services and false hopes.

- Even in their recreation, let them be excessive with working out, hunting, fishing, yoga, sports and more sports. Have them return from their recreation exhausted, stressed, and less time for faith and family.

- When they go to church, involve them in gossip and small talk, and make them bored so their minds wander off to all the things and activities they have become addicted to. They'll keep checking their watches, wishing the service to hurry up and be over. That way they won't experience Jesus while they are there.

INTERESTING, ISN'T IT?

Like I said before, Evil wants us to doubt and deny its existence, because by doing so, it renders us powerless over it and gives it free reign to complete its agenda.

Somehow I believe we all know it is real because of our inability to wrap our minds around genocide, mass murders, rape, child abuse, torture, beheading which even the media labels "demonic."

This core belief and response to Evil is in us, because despite being influenced and infected by it, we are still beings of **Light**, connected to God, which enables us to recognize both Good and Evil—in this case, Evil.

The Word of God describes these beings, entities or powers as the real Enemy.

- "Our battle is not against flesh and blood, but against Powers, Principalities, and Rulers from the Kingdom of Darkness." (Eph. 6:12)

- "When you pray, say, Our Father who art in Heaven...**Deliver Us From Evil.**" (Mt. 6:13)

- "These are the signs that will follow all those who believe, whomever they lay their hands on will be healed... In my name, they will cast out demons and spirits." (Mk. 16:17)

STOP:

The above words of God and Jesus are critical for all who read this book and for all of humanity. Read them again one more time before proceeding.

The reason they are critical is Jesus overcame Satan's

temptations of power and greed when He was tempted in the desert. When He was condemned, scourged, and crucified, He overcame the temptation of doubt, despair, fear of Suffering and Death. He did so by **choosing to focus on His Father**, moment by moment instead of the temptation and suffering. Then He **chose from moment to moment with His WILL** to Trust His Father.

Just as Jesus conquered Evil through the power of His Will and Trust while in a flesh and blood body like ours He has paved the way and shown us what to do, how to attack, defeat, and deliver ourselves and others from Evil.

- **The power that is in us now is greater than the powers that are in the world. (Eph. 1:19)**

Do you believe this? More importantly have you experienced the Lord's power that is greater than the evil you face?

I thought at this time it would be helpful to clarify the difference between **Deliverance and Possession**, which I have found very confusing to people when talking about or experiencing evil spirits and powers.

I found the following psychological descriptions of conditions and accompanying manifestations. In addition to defining them, they also offer answers and therapeutic guidelines in dealing with the people who are experiencing these phenomena. Being in the deliverance ministry, I have found them to be very helpful in developing an appropriate spiritual and psychological approach when ministering with a person for their deliverance

OPPRESSION – OBSESSION - POSSESSION

PSYCHO-SPIRITUAL TERMS for the conditions, less than Possession, that respond to the commands of authority to dispel forces of Evil are called Oppression and Obsession.

In a state of **OPPRESSION**, people experience attacks of evil spirit from outside of themselves. The most common characteristic of oppression is a sense of heaviness about the head. Frequently people find it difficult to think out a situation or persevere in a task. They feel discouraged and impeded by alien pressures; that is, forces not coming from within themselves.

Such persons alone, or in prayer with another, should command in the name of Jesus that the spirit of oppression leave and not return.

In the case of **OBSESSION**, the evil spirits are in a position to create severe disturbances in a particular area within a person. There is an actual presence within the person, though. That presence is **NOT** in a position to control the person. The person can still exercise free will in determining his or her life. The person can also expel the evil spirits, though often, another person is necessary to assist or direct the deliverance. The person ministering deliverance should have the obsessed person utilize as much spiritual authority as possible. In obsession, the goal is to have the person obsessed arrive at the point of repenting of all past sins and present sinful attitudes, renounce the spirit obsessing them and with the minister, command such spirit or spirits in the name of Jesus to depart and not return.

Put simply, P**OSSESSION** is a person who has lost their Will completely and the power to choose. The spirit, entity, or demon(s) are in total control of the person, able to manifest their demonic powers. For practical purposes, the Ritual of Exorcism is reserved (by the local bishop), at least in the Catholic Tradition, to an appointed trained "Exorcist." An "Exorcist" is needed, because a possessed person has **no Will** left that is functioning. This is unlike deliverance where the person prays and works together with others to deliver themselves, as suggested in the case of **OBSESSION.**

***Good News: If you think you are possessed, you are NOT.**

BOTH OPPRESSION AND OBSESSION may require a physical examination and psychiatric assessment to deal with personal issues for the deliverance and healing to take place. Specific diseases, like Parkinson's disease, can cause certain psychotic manifestations as well as chemical deficiencies. Both have medical therapy treatments. This is why before praying for deliverance, I ask the person if they have talked to a medical doctor or psychiatrist about their experience. In other words, don't assume that evil spirits are attacking the person or entities no matter what they see or hear. If you do assume that and jump right in praying for deliverance, this may be counter-productive by falsely suggesting and confirming that the person is experiencing the demonic and may even be possessed. **NOT GOOD**!

***CAUTION**:
With all this talk about Evil and Deliverance, don't start

looking for Satan and Evil in everything and everybody. Evil loves your attention and curiosity. Do not give it one iota of your attention. Keep your focus and attention on the Lord with you, and if you feel tempted or finding yourself thinking about it too much, simply tell it to "Get lost in the name of Jesus" and forget about it

JESUS:
- "The power that is in You now is greater than the powers that are in the world."

- "While you are in the world you will suffer, but don't be afraid of it or let your hearts be troubled, because **I overcame my fear of it and so can you**, because I am with you now."

- You will hear these Scriptures repeated often while reading this Manual because they are essential for you to not only remember them, but also call them to mind regularly. Try to memorize them and train your brain to use them to dispel your fears and worries.

CHAPTER 5
EXORCISM IN THE CATHOLIC CHURCH
From Wikipedia, the free encyclopedia

(The following is from Wikipedia and an explanation of Demonic Possession and the Teaching of the Catholic Church and the Role of the Exorcist and procedure.)

The Catholic Church authorizes the use of exorcism for those who are believed to be the victims of demonic possession. In Roman Catholicism, exorcism is sacramental but not a sacrament, unlike baptism or confession. Unlike a sacrament, exorcism "integrity and efficacy do not depend ... on the rigid use of an unchanging formula or on the ordered sequence of prescribed actions. Its efficacy depends on two elements: authorization from valid and licit Church authorities, and the faith of the exorcist."

The Catechism of the Catholic Church states: "When the Church asks publicly and authoritatively in the name of Jesus Christ that a person or object be protected against the power of the Evil One and withdrawn from his dominion, it is called exorcism."

The Catholic Church revised the Rite of Exorcism in January 1999, though the traditional Rite of Exorcism in Latin is allowed as an option. The ritual assumes that possessed persons retain their free will, though the demon may hold control over their physical body, and involves prayers, blessings, and invocations with the use of the document Of Exorcisms and Certain Supplications.

Solemn exorcisms, according to the Canon law of the Church, can be exercised only by an ordained priest (or higher prelate), with the express permission of the local bishop, and only after a careful medical examination to exclude the possibility of mental illness.

Catholic Encyclopedia (1908) enjoined: "Superstition ought not to be confounded with religion, however much their history may be interwoven, nor magic, however white it may be, with a legitimate religious Rite." By the late 1960s, Roman Catholic exorcisms were seldom performed in the United States, but by the mid-1970s, popular film and literature revived interest in the ritual, with thousands claiming demonic possession.

Maverick priests who belonged to fringes took advantage of the increase in demand and performed exorcisms with little or no official sanction. The exorcisms that they performed were, according to Contemporary American Religion, "clandestine, underground affairs, undertaken without the approval of the Catholic Church and without the rigorous psychological screening that the church required. In subsequent years, the Church took more aggressive action on the demon-expulsion front.

The practice of exorcism without consent from the Catholic Church is what prompted the official guidelines from 1614 to be amended. The amendment established the procedure that clergy members and each individual who claims to be impacted by demonic possession must follow. This includes the rule that the potentially possessed individual must be evaluated by a medical professional before any other acts are taken.

The primary reason for this action is to eliminate any suspicion of mental illness, before the next steps of the procedure are taken. Since demonic possession was extremely rare, and mental health issues are often mistaken for demonic possession, the Vatican requires that each diocese have a specially trained priest who is able to diagnose demonic possession and perform exorcisms when necessary. In more recent years, the number of exorcisms has increased, and all dioceses are now required by the Vatican to have a trained exorcist available as needed.

WHEN AN EXORCISM IS NEEDED

According to the Vatican guidelines issued in 1999, "the person who claims to be possessed must be evaluated by doctors to rule out a mental or physical illness." Most reported cases do not require an exorcism because twentieth-century Catholic officials regard genuine demonic possession as an extremely rare phenomenon that is easily confounded with natural mental disturbances. Despite that fact, every diocese is required to have at least one priest that is an exorcist, or is trained to perform exorcisms.

As the demand for exorcisms has increased over the past few decades, the number of trained exorcists has also risen. In prior times, exorcists were kept fairly anonymous, and the performance of exorcisms remained a secret.

Many times a person just needs spiritual or medical help, especially if drugs or other addictions are present. The specially trained priest and medical professionals will be able to work together to address the patient, and be able to determine what type of illness the patient is suffering from. After the need of the person has been determined then the appropriate help will be met. In offering spiritual help prayers may be offered, the laying on of hands or a counseling session may be prescribed. The exorcist may not perform an exorcism if he does not know the person.

SIGNS OF DEMONIC POSSESSION

Signs of demonic invasion vary depending on the type of demon and its purpose, including:

- **Speaking or understanding another language which they had never learned before**

- **Intense hatred and violent reaction toward all religious objects or items**

- **Antipathy towards entering a church, speaking Jesus' name or hearing scripture.**

- **Knowledge of things that are distant or hidden**

- Supernatural physical strength not subject to the person's build or age

- Loss or lack of appetite

- Cutting, scratching, and biting of skin

- A cold feeling in the room

- Unnatural bodily postures and change in the person's face and body

- Losing control of their normal personality and entering into a frenzy or rage, and/or attacking others

- Change in the person's voice

- Prediction of future events (sometimes through dreams)

- Levitation and moving of objects / things

PROCESS OF THE EXORCISM

In the process of an exorcism the person possessed may be restrained so that they do not harm themselves or any person present. The exorcist then prays and commands for the demons to retreat. The Catholic Priest recites certain prayers, the Our Father, Hail Mary, and the Athanasian Creed. Exorcists follow procedures listed in the Ritual of the exorcism revised by the Vatican in 1999. Seasoned exorcists use the **Rituale Romanum** as a starting point, not always following the prescribed formula exactly

THE GALE ENCYCLOPEDIA OF THE UNUSUAL

Gale describes that an exorcism was a **confrontation** and **not simply a prayer** and once it has begun it has to finish no matter how long it takes. If the exorcist stops the rite, then the demon will pursue him which is why the process being brought to completion is so essential. After the exorcism has been finished the person possessed feels a "kind of release of guilt and feels reborn and freed of sin." Not all exorcisms are successful the first time; it could take days, weeks, or months of constant prayer and exorcisms.

CHAPTER 6
DELIVERANCE RITUALS

IMPORTANT: The following are Rituals for Deliverance, **NOT** Exorcism. When using any of these rituals, you need to apply an "attitude." Do **NOT** show any signs of FEAR, no matter what you see, hear or feel. It's OK to be startled, but immediately respond by focusing on Jesus with you, then get in there and attack. When you are done attacking, attack again, and punish them with the name and blood of Jesus until they leave. The more you do it, the easier it gets and they will be afraid of you, instead of you them.

REMEMBER, don't be looking for Evil in everybody or everywhere. Keep your focus on the Lord and His Will. Oh yea, and enjoy life.

DELIVERANCE RITUAL #1
(Simple deliverance)

Jesus, bind and cast out who ever and whatever this Evil is with Your name and the blood You shed on the Cross. I command you, Evil, to leave. Jesus is the Lord of my Life. Amen.

DELIVERANCE RITUAL #2
(For minor attacks of oppression and for obsession)

In your name, Jesus and by the blood You shed on the cross for me, the Power and authority of the Holy Spirit, and through the intercession of you, Blessed Mother and St. Michael the Archangel, bind Satan and all evil spirits and powers attacking me. Punish them and cast them out.

I bind and cast you out and command you to go before the throne of God, your creator, to do with you as He wills.

Lord, grant me the grace to keep my attention on You here with me and not take back these temptations and lies by thinking about or dwelling on them.

I am a child of God. I belong to You Jesus and You alone. You are the Lord of my life. Into Your hands, I commend my spirit.

Response: "Deliver me, Lord"

FROM:

Fear and Anger...	"Deliver me, Lord"
Pride and Self-Righteousness...	"Deliver me, Lord"
Greed and Selfishness...	"Deliver me, Lord"
Envy and Jealousy...	"Deliver me, Lord"
Lust and Desires of the Flesh...	"Deliver me, Lord"
Hatred and Judging...	"Deliver me, Lord"

Depression and Loneliness...	"Deliver me, Lord"
Doubt and Despair...	"Deliver me, Lord"
Self-Hatred...	"Deliver me, Lord"

Replacing You, Lord, and my church family with my desires for things and doing only what I want, instead of your will... **"Deliver me, Lord"**

RENEWAL OF MY BAPTISMAL PROMISES

- I surrender my entire mind, body, and spirit to You, Jesus, my Lord and Savior and no other.

- I refuse to be mastered by Sin and Evil.

- I renounce you, Satan, and all of your lies and empty promises.

- I bind and cast you out by my love for Jesus.

OUR FATHER who art in Heaven, hallowed be Thy name. Thy Kingdom come, Thy will be done, on Earth as it is in Heaven. Give me this day, my daily bread, and forgive me my trespasses as I forgive those who trespass against me. And lead me out of temptation and **DELIVER ME FROM EVIL**. Amen.

Glory to You, my Creator and Father, and to my Lord and Friend, Jesus the Christ, and You the Holy Spirit, the Unconditional Love and Wisdom of God as it was in the beginning, is now, and ever shall be. AMEN.

(If you are attacked again, you attack and torture Evil, whoever and whatever they are with the above prayers until they leave. Then go and enjoy life, because the reason He gives us power over temptation and Evil is to have JOY, LIFE and PEACE, **so get to it!**)

DELIVERANCE RITUAL #3
(For those evil spirits and demons that require more prayer and fasting)

STRONGLY SUGGESTED: Bring others possessing deep faith with you to pray this Ritual (A Pastor or people with the gift of Discernment and the deliverance ministry)

PRAYER OF PROTECTION

Jesus, through the intercession of the Blessed Mother, St. Michael the Archangel, the Apostles, Martyrs and Saints, and by the authority of the Holy Catholic Church, we ask You for your protection from all the wickedness, evil, and harm to our bodies, minds, and souls by Satan and all evil powers, rulers, principalities, demons and spirits.

Grant us the wisdom of the Holy Spirit to guide us through and to the completion of your Will to cast out all evil from _____ We ask this in Your name Jesus and Your precious blood, that it be poured over all of us with your protection, love, wisdom and power. Amen.

INVOKING THE HOLY SPIRIT

(Shared and spontaneous praises invoking the Holy Spirit to be the director of the deliverance are offered at this time. Those with the gift of tongues should use their gift. Others are invited to sing or recite the following.)

(Sing or Recite)

> Spirit of the Living God,
> Fall afresh on me.
> Spirit of the Living God, Fall afresh on me.
> Melt me, Mold me, Use me, Fill me.
> Spirit of the Living God
> Fall afresh on me
> **(Repeat)**

PRAYER OF CONFESSION AND FORGIVENESS

Response: Lord, forgive me.

Lord, if I have:

- Spent less and less time with you and drifted away from my church family... Lord, forgive me!

- Judged, gossiped, and hurt others... R.

- Lusted, watched pornography and used others sexually... R.

- Been in unhealthy relationships... R.

- Held grudges and wanted to hurt someone... R.

- Been involved in any occult practices and rituals, or with people involved with these evil powers... R.

- Been selfish, greedy, and have not participated in

service ministry for the poor, sick, and the marginalized... R.

- Allowed Evil to attach itself to my body, mind and spirit, because of the pleasure and the power it gave me... R.

- Abused alcohol, drugs, and prescription medications... R.

- Abused and been used by others... R.

PRAYER FOR POWER OF DELIVERANCE

Lord God, our Almighty Father, You who created us, and You our Lord and Friend, Jesus the Christ, as you gave to your holy apostles and disciples the power to cast out and trample on Satan, serpents and evil spirits grant to us that same power and authority as we deliver_____ from any and all evil. **Amen.**

PRAYER OF DELIVERANCE

Response: In the name of Jesus, I cast you out.

- All powers, principalities, rulers from the kingdom of darkness... In the name of Jesus, I cast you out.

- The spirits in charge in this oppression, obsession, and infestation... R.

- Spirits and demons of fear and lies...   R.

- Spirits and demons of lust, sex abuse and rape... R.

- Spirits and demons of violence and hatred...

- Spirits and demons of physical abuse... R.

- All demons, spirits, powers of addiction and disease that have a hold on_____'s body, mind, feelings and will... R.

- All contacts and participation in occult practices, rituals, curses, witchcraft, use of articles of darkness and evil... R.

(Hold a crucifix and sprinkle holy water in four directions. And in a commanding voice read the following)

I cast out every unclean spirit, every Satanic power, every attack of the powers of darkness, every legion and principality, in the name of my Lord Jesus Christ.

JESUS POUR YOUR BLOOD ON, TORTURE, AND PUNISH

- Semjasa, Azezal, Leaders of the fallen angels and their cohorts.

- All of them—their children with human women, the Nephilim, the giants, and Satan himself.

- The fallen angels that desecrated, brought sin and death to us and all physical reality.

- All the powers, rulers and false gods from ancient times until the present.

- Babylonian evil demons and spirits that have sprung from there, Ahab, Jezebel, Leviathan, Nimrod, All the powers, principalities, rulers, demons and spirits of Babylon, Sumer, Akkadia, Sodom and Gamorrah.

THE HOLY SPIRIT CRUSHES you Satan and all evil demons and spirits with the knowledge and truth of your future and eternal damnation.

- For all eternity you will dwell in darkness with no experience or hope of light that you betrayed and lost.

- For all eternity, you have lost your former state.

- For all eternity, you will experience pain, but your bodies will not die.

- For all eternity, you will be imprisoned in hell without hope.

- For all eternity you will experience no love, no power, no pleasure, and no light, only darkness and despair.

- For all eternity, you will live in chaos and destroy one another without end.

- For all eternity, you are damned, cursed, despised, and powerless.

- For all eternity, you will be tortured, tormented, experience all the horrific suffering you caused humanity from the beginning.

- For all eternity, you will never see or experience God or the light of divinity.

- You will lose all the divine knowledge that you infected humanity with.

- You will rot in the very evil you created and without escape.

THE HOLY SPIRIT

- Binds your displays of tricks and antics.
- Binds and casts you out.
- Compels you to never come back, oppress or obsess _____.

- Breaks all gates, links, and pathways to your hierarchy of evil from the least of spirits to Satan.

- Tortures, scourges, and causes you the greatest pain and suffering to all evil that is present here.

ST. MICHAEL AND WARRIOR ANGELS
- Pierce you with the sword of the truth.
- Bind and cast you out.
- Command you to accept defeat and leave, or your punishment will continue.

BLESSED MOTHER,

Mother of our Lord and Savior Jesus the Christ, you who stood before the beast who was ready to devour your child, but you gave birth to the Son of God who conquered our fears, temptation, sin, and death itself, destroy, bind, cast out, and deliver this child of God from all evil including the beast that Jesus condemned to the fires of hell.

- **Hail Mary full of grace..... Amen.**

ALL YOU SAINTS AND HOLY ONES

By the authority of the Church and all believers, deliver and punish Satan and Evil that is present here with the light of your faith and love for the Father, Son, and Holy Spirit.

Response: Punishes and casts you out.
- Light of St. Clare... R.
- Light of St. Francis... R.
- Light of St. Benedict... R.
- Light of St. Anthony... R..
- All the Angels, Martyrs, and Saints ... R.

- The Holy Catholic Church and all of God's children... R

<u>THE RESURRECTION CASTS YOU OUT</u>
- The Resurrection destroyed your powers of fear, sin, and death.

- The Resurrection raises us to the heights of Heaven as the Father's children.

- The Resurrection will torment you now and forever with the knowledge that God has given to us what you never had and will never know or experience for all eternity.

- You who seduced and experimented with our physical bodies and minds and brought sin, suffering, and death into the world and us has now been undone by Christ's Resurrection.

- The Resurrection casts you out with the knowledge of what you lost for lust and power, and condemned yourselves for all eternity. You are the most stupid and pathetic of all created beings.

- The blood of Christ and His Resurrection breaks and destroys all bonds, legal rights and holds on mind, body and soul, back to 10 generations of _____.

- Your time here Satan is over. We will continue to torture you until you leave

RENEWAL OF OUR BAPTISMAL PROMISES

Lord, grant our sister/brother peace, Unconditional Love, and fill them with the Holy Spirit as together we renew our baptismal promises, renouncing Satan, all evil, and profess our faith and love for you, Father, Son, and Holy Spirit.

V. Do we renounce you, Satan?
R. We do.

V. And all your works.
R. We do.

V. And all of your empty promises.
R. We do.

V. Do we renounce sin, so as to live in the freedom of the children of God?
R. We do.

V. Do we renounce the lure of evil, so that sin may have no mastery over us?
R. We do.

V. Do we renounce Satan, the author and prince of sin?
R. We do.

V. Do we believe in God, the Father Almighty, Creator of Heaven and Earth?
R. We do.

V. Do we believe in Jesus Christ, His only Son, our Lord who was born of the Virgin Mary, suffered death, was buried, rose again from the dead, and is seated at the right

hand of the Father?
R. We do

V. Do we believe in the Holy Spirit, the Holy Catholic Church, the communion of saints, the forgiveness of sins, the resurrection of the body, and life everlasting?
R. We do.

Our Father... Amen.

(Sprinkle all with holy water)

Lord, bless, watch over and protect _____ his/her house, family, and all of us, in the name of the Father, Son and Holy Spirit. Amen.

EXORCISM OF A HOUSE
Breaking Household Curses and Spells

In the name and the blood of You, our Lord Jesus Christ, through the intercession of the Blessed Virgin Mary, Blessed Michael the Archangel, and the Blessed Apostles and all the Saints, we ask, that you break and dissolve any and all curses, hexes, spells, seals, satanic vows and pacts, spiritual bonding and soul ties with satanic forces, evil wishes, evil desires, hereditary seals, snares, traps, lies, obstacles, deceptions, diversions, spiritual influences, and every dysfunction and disease from any source whatsoever, that have been placed upon this house and those who reside here.

HOUSE BLESSING:

(While using Holy Water and incense if available, go through the house blessing each room, casting out all evil and placing them under the authority and protection of Jesus)

Father in Heaven, please rebuke these evil spirits and their effects and cast them away from all the rooms of this house and those who reside here so that they may live in their home in Peace, unmolested, and live according to Your Will for Your Greater Glory.

CLOSING PRAYER:

(Join hands in a circle, end by shouting the Our Father and looking around at each other. Jesus said, "Love dispels Fear." As you look around, your love for each other will deliver you from your fear, now, and whenever you are tempted to be afraid.)

OUR FATHER.... Amen!

FINAL BLESSING:

May You almighty God bless us and remain with us, in the name of the Father, Son, and the Holy Spirit, AMEN!

(With your Thumb, trace the sign of the cross on each other's forehead and offer some sign of affection and peace.)

"**Do not be afraid any more**. I am with you and will never abandon you, so do not abandon Me. Call on me and together we will attack Satan again and the Evil that is attacking you."

CHAPTER 7
FINAL THOUGHTS IN PRAYING FOR DELIVERANCE

- Focus off the evil you are experiencing.

- Focus off any disturbing actions and antics of demons and spirits.

- If you are seeing or hearing anything that frightens you, immediately say **"NO"** to the evil presence and fear.

- With your whole being and Will focus on Jesus right there with you by saying "Lord, are you ready?"

- Trust me from my years of deliverance ministry, He is there with you, ready, locked and loaded.

- Then use the short Ritual #1, take the offensive and attack, and keep attacking by praising the Lord and expressing your faith, love, and trust in Him. Pray also to the Blessed Mother and St. Michael the archangel to intercede and attack with you.

- For more intense encounters with evil, check with your doctor and psychologist to see if it's a medical or a mental problem that can be solved with medication and counseling.

- Once it is determined that it's not physical (medical) or mental, then find a pastor or educated groups experienced in the deliverance ministry to attack with you using the **Deliverance Ritual #3**.

TAKE THE OFFENSIVE:

- **Get an attitude.**

- You command and tell them what to do and what Jesus and you are going to do to them.

- Make fun of them, their antics, tricks, and threats (they hate that).

- Call them names: ugly, pathetic, losers and a joke... etc.

- Threaten them with the truth and their future in hell where they will experience eternal pain, suffering, and everything they did to individual people and humanity.

- Remind them that the greatest suffering for them will be that there is not only no escape, but **no coffee breaks.**

- Remind them of your future when Jesus raises you up from your suffering and dead body that they corrupted and leads you to eternal life in heaven.

- Remind them you are not just a creation of God like they are, but you are God's children that they never were or will be.

- Remind them while they are in Hell forever, **you** will never again be afraid, suffer and die, and never be aware of Evil or them.

GOOD NEWS: Keep doing this and little by little you will no longer be afraid of evil or their antics and tricks, surprised and startled maybe, but they in fact will be afraid of **you** as they were and are of Jesus.

REMEMBER: Don't look for evil everywhere and in everything. Much of evil comes from you and me in our own thinking, decisions and actions.

REMEMBER: Just because you now know how and what to do about evil doesn't mean that you won't continue to be tempted and attacked as long as you are in your physical body, which is their turf.

REJOICE, that you are now in the great army of the Lord, with the Blessed Mother, St. Michael the archangel, his warrior angels, and the saints.

St. Paul said: **"Put on the Armor of Christ"**

HERE IS YOUR ARMOR: For Protection and Attacking

- The Holy Spirit
- The Name of Jesus
- The Blood of Jesus
- The Word of God and The Truth
- The Blessed Mother, St. Michael, his Holy Angels and the Saints
- Your Faith And Trust In The Lord To depend on all the above

DELIVERANCE REQUEST QUESTIONNAIRE

(I am including the following questionnaire that I have given to Parish and Chancery receptionists to use when fielding a call from someone who is seeking help to deal with experiencing Evil, seeing objects, entities, hearing unusual sounds and voices, objects moving or being thrown, etc.)

Name:_____

Address:_____

Phone: _____

INITIAL QUESTIONS:

When did this start? How Long ago?
_____

Are you seeing or hearing anything?   **YES   NO**

If so what? _____

Have you seen your medical doctor about this?
YES NO

Have you contacted a priest or anyone, to help you deal with this problem?

YES NO

If so, who? Name/s

_____   _____

Have you spoken to a Counselor
YES NO

If so, who? Name/s

_____

_____

Sometimes what you are experiencing may be physical, and only requires medication. Certain diseases and psychological conditions can cause what you are experiencing, and could be diagnosed and treated.

By seeing a Medical doctor, and a Psychiatrist, would help determine if what you are experiencing, is of a spiritual nature. When you find out the results, you can call us back, and the Diocese will appoint a priest to contact and assist you in a prayer of Deliverance.

Until then, I am going to send you some information that will help you pray and ask the Lord to deliver you from any Evil that you are experiencing, and frightening you.

(Send Ritual #1 and #2 with description of how evil works)

Thank you for calling, and know that you are not alone in this, because the Lord and we are with you and will be praying for you.

IS JESUS CALLING YOU?
Jesus Sends Out the Seventy-Two Disciples

- "After this the Lord appointed seventy-two others and sent them two by two ahead of him to every town and place where he was about to go...."

- The seventy-two returned with joy and said, "Lord, even the demons submit to us in your name." (Luke 10:1-23, NIV)

- "He replied, "I saw Satan fall like lightning from heaven. I have given you authority to trample on snakes and scorpions and to overcome all the power of the enemy; nothing will harm you. However, do not rejoice that the spirits submit to you, but rejoice that your names are written in heaven."

Now that you have read this manual, seriously consider helping people who are frightened, angry, or hate themselves because of their sins.

Trust me, many of your friends and acquaintances, as well as yourself are attacked by **FEAR** every day. From what Jesus has taught you in this manual realize that they suffer unnecessarily and are alone in dealing with it.

Step out in faith and tell them Jesus can and wants to deliver them and that you know how.

Then, tell them to close their eyes, put your hand on their head or shoulder, and slowly pray **Ritual #1.**

and simply end with a **Prayer to St. Michael**, a **Hail Mary**, and **Our Father**. You will be amazed what Jesus can do through your faith and trust.

Just think of the great gift you are learning that you can give to your family, loved ones and friends who are frightened, worried and suffering.

Jesus might just be hoping you will ask for this gift.

MY PRAYER FOR YOU

Lord,
Watch over, protect, empower all those who read this Manual. When confronted by Evil, deliver them from their Fear quickly, and grant them the grace to call on the power of your Name and the Blood you shed on the cross, to conquer the Evil that is attacking and tempting them. Give them the faith to make a choice to Trust and have the strength to not give in to fear and doubt. Amen

"The Lord is with you. Now, go Attack and Torture Satan and the Evil that brought suffering and death to the World, Humanity, Your Loved Ones, and You"

Fr. Francis Pompei ofm

"Don't be Afraid! I am with you!"

Fr. Francis Pompei ofm
A Franciscan Friar of Holy Name Province
AUTHOR

CREDITS

- Parable 'Busy', Andrus ,"BUSY." https://www.sermoncentral.com/sermons/not-around-but- through-Joe-Harding-sermon-on-endurance- 35616?ref=Sermon Serps

- Definitions of Seances, Divination, Satanism, Spells, etc., paraphrased from Exepedia.

- Jesus on Cover, Mary Jo Woyciesjes (Artist)

- Book of Enoch, Johnson, Ken. (2012) Ancient Book of Enoch. Create Space Independent Publishing Platform

- The Catholic Church and Exorcism, Wikipedia

- Scripture, New American Bible, NIV

www.ingramcontent.com/pod-product-compliance
Lightning Source LLC
Chambersburg PA
CBHW050445010526
44118CB00013B/1688